TOUR GUIDE TO EXETER: Exploring the City Hidden Gems

CALEB SMULT

GRATITUDE

I want to take a moment to express my sincere gratitude for choosing my book 'Tour Guide to Exeter(UK)'. It warms my heart to know that you have chosen my book to explore the beautiful city of Exeter in the United Kingdom.

As a lover of this city, I have made it my mission to share the hidden gems and must-see sights through the pages of my book. I want to make sure that your experience in Exeter is not just a tourist visit but one that immerses you into the essence and soul of this wonderful place.

In this book, you will find a comprehensive guide of the most interesting and fascinating attractions in Exeter, along with useful tips on where to eat, stay, and what to do. I hope that it will make your trip to Exeter easier and more enjoyable.

Once again, thank you for your support and for choosing my book. I believe that it will be an excellent companion during your visit to Exeter. I wish you an unforgettable experience in the city and hope that this book will make your trip even more special.

Copyright © 2024, Caleb Smult.

This work and its content are protected under international copyright laws.

No part of this publication may be reproduced, distributed, or transmitted in any form or by any means, including photocopying, recording, or other electronic or mechanical methods, without the prior written permission of the author, except in the case of brief quotations embodied in critical reviews and certain other noncommercial uses permitted by copyright law.

TABLE OF CONTENTS

PART 1: DISCOVERING EXETER

1. INTRODUCTION TO EXETER
 A WARM WELCOME TO EXETER
 UNRAVELING THE CHARMS OF EXETER

2. HISTORY OF EXETER
 FROM ANCIENT ROOTS TO MODERN MARVELS
 TRACING EXETER'S RICH HERITAGE

3. EXETER TODAY
 VIBRANT CULTURE AND CONTEMPORARY LIFE
 EMBRACING TRADITION AMIDST MODERNITY

PART 2: GETTING TO KNOW EXETER

4. PLANNING YOUR TRIP
 PREPARING FOR YOUR EXETER ADVENTURE
 BEST TIMES TO VISIT EXETER

5. GETTING TO EXETER
 NAVIGATING TRANSPORTATION OPTIONS
 TIPS FOR HASSLE-FREE TRAVEL TO EXETER

6. GETTING AROUND EXETER

EXPLORING THE CITY'S LAYOUT
TRANSPORTATION WITHIN EXETER

PART 3: EXPERIENCING EXETER

7. LANDMARKS AND ATTRACTIONS
MUST-SEE SIGHTS IN EXETER
HIDDEN GEMS WAITING TO BE DISCOVERED

8. CULTURAL EXPERIENCES
DIVING INTO EXETER'S CULTURAL SCENE
IMMERSING YOURSELF IN LOCAL TRADITIONS

9. OUTDOOR ADVENTURES
NATURE ESCAPES IN AND AROUND EXETER
THRILLING OUTDOOR ACTIVITIES FOR EVERY ADVENTURER

PART 4: LIVING IN EXETER

10. ACCOMMODATION OPTIONS
FINDING YOUR HOME AWAY FROM HOME
ACCOMMODATION CHOICES FOR EVERY BUDGET

11. DINING AND SHOPPING
SAVORY DELIGHTS AND CULINARY JOURNEYS

SHOPPING EXPERIENCES IN EXETER

PART 5: EXPLORING BEYOND EXETER

12. DAY TRIPS AND EXCURSIONS
 VENTURING BEYOND THE CITY LIMITS
 UNVEILING EXETER'S SURROUNDING WONDERS

13. NEARBY ATTRACTIONS
 DISCOVERING GEMS NEAR EXETER
 ITINERARIES FOR UNFORGETTABLE DAY TRIPS

PART 6: PRACTICALITIES

14. ESSENTIAL TIPS FOR VISITORS
 HANDY ADVICE FOR A SMOOTH STAY
 PRACTICAL INFORMATION TO KEEP IN MIND

15. SUSTAINABLE TRAVEL IN EXETER
 SUPPORTING RESPONSIBLE TOURISM INITIATIVES
 ECO-FRIENDLY PRACTICES FOR CONSCIOUS TRAVELERS

16. CONCLUSION

PART 1: DISCOVERING EXETER

1. INTRODUCTION TO EXETER

A WARM WELCOME TO EXETER

Welcome to Exeter, where you can hear whispers of history and feel the warmth of the present.

As you set foot in Exeter, prepare for an excursion like no other. It is a gold mine of stories, hanging tight for you to make a plunge and reveal its insider facts. Picture yourself walking around the interesting roads, feeling the beat of the city underneath your feet. You'll find comfortable bistros welcoming you in for a cuppa and distinctive shops enticing you with their products. What's more, goodness, the food! Prepare to tempt your taste buds with a gastronomic experience through our different culinary scene.

However, there's something else! Exeter isn't just about the metropolitan hurrying around. Step outside and you'll be welcomed by the magnificence of the natural environmental elements. Whether you love a relaxed stroll along the riverbanks or an enjoying a hike through the open country, nature's jungle gym is right at your doorstep.

So go on, embrace the soul of experience and allow Exeter to wind its wizardry around you. Maybe coming around for a day or seven days, we guarantee you an encounter you will always remember. Welcome to Exeter, let the experience start!

UNRAVELING THE CHARMS OF EXETER

Exeter offers an enamoring blend of old tourist spots, beautiful scenes, and an enthusiastic local area soul that charms guests from all edges of the globe. Below are highlighted the charms embedded in Exeter.

Rich History and Heritage

Exeter's set of experiences goes back more than 2,000 years, apparent in its Roman walls, archaic structures, and Gothic basilica. Explore the famous Exeter House of God, a magnum opus of engineering that overwhelms the horizon with its staggering vaulted roofs and multifaceted stained glass windows. Meander through the city's tight archaic roads, where each corner uncovers stories of fights, exchange, and the versatility of its kin through hundreds of years of progress.

Social Hub

Beyond its verifiable charm, Exeter is a flourishing social hub. Find exhibitions displaying modern art, theaters facilitating varied exhibitions, and galleries offering bits of knowledge into history and worldwide impacts. The Royal Albert Memorial Museum, lovingly known as RAMM, houses a mother lode of relics from around the world, while the Exeter Phoenix gives a stage to innovative expressions and innovative articulation.

Quayside Charm

Move back from the clamor of the downtown area and track down serenity along Exeter Quayside. River Exe wanders delicately, previous notable distribution centers changed into enchanting bistros, bars, and stores. Partake in a relaxed walk or boat trip along the waterway, absorbing all encompassing perspectives and the quiet feel that characterizes this waterside region.

Green Spaces and Outside Adventures

Nature lovers will find a lot to explore in Exeter's green spaces and outside adventures. From the grounds of Northernhay Gardens, one of Britain's most established national gardens, to the rough excellence of Dartmoor National Park a short drive away, open air devotees can climb, cycle, or just loosen up in the midst of nature's magnificence.

Culinary Delights

No visit to Exeter is completed without examining its culinary delight. Enjoy neighborhood fortes, for example, Devonshire cream tea with newly heated scones, or savor seafood caught from nearby coastal waters.. From customary bars serving good feasts to grant winning eateries pushing culinary limits, Exeter takes special care of each and every sense of taste and inclination.

Warm Hospitality

Most importantly, Exeter invites guests with warm hospitality and a sense of the society. Whether you're exploring its noteworthy destinations, perusing craftsman markets, or just visiting with local people in a local bistro, you'll find a city that embraces its past while embracing what's in store.

As you set out on your journey to unwind the charms of Exeter, plan to be enamored by its rich history, dynamic culture, and pleasant scenes. Prepare to fully explore, find, and fall in love with Exeter; a city that welcomes you to compose your own part in its celebrated heritage.

2. HISTORY OF EXETER

FROM ANCIENT ROOTS TO MODERN MARVELS

Let's take a journey through time, from the ancient roots to the modern marvels that shape the captivating history of Exeter.

Centuries ago, Exeter was a bustling Roman town known as Isca Dumnoniorum. Imagine Roman soldiers marching through the streets, merchants selling their wares in the markets, and citizens going about their daily lives within the protective walls of the city. As the centuries passed, Exeter evolved into a prosperous city, with its iconic cathedral standing as a testament to its enduring heritage. Picture knights in shining armor, lords and ladies hosting grand feasts, and craftsmen creating intricate works of art within the city's bustling workshops.

Exeter's history isn't just about the distant past; it's a story of resilience and adaptation in the face of change. The city weathered Viking invasions, Civil War sieges, and devastating fires, yet it rose from the ashes each time, stronger and more vibrant than before. Now in the modern era, Exeter has transformed into a thriving hub of commerce, culture, and innovation. Its streets are lined with shops, cafes, and businesses, while its universities and research institutions attract scholars and students from around the world.

Yet amidst the hustle and bustle of modern life, traces of Exeter's ancient roots can still be found. From the Roman walls that encircle the city to the medieval guildhalls that dot the skyline, reminders of the past are everywhere, woven seamlessly into the fabric of everyday life. So next time you wander through the streets of Exeter, take a moment to appreciate the journey that brought us from ancient roots to modern marvels. It's a history worth celebrating, and a legacy that continues to shape the city we know and love today.

TRACING EXETER'S RICH HERITAGE

Diving into the fullness of Exeter's legacy, where each stone recounts a story and each corner holds a piece of history.

Envision strolling through the cobbled roads of Exeter, encompassed by old structures that have represented hundreds of years. These structures aren't simply blocks and mortar; they're time cases, saving the recollections and customs of previous eras.

One of the royal gems of Exeter's heritage is its great church. Standing gladly at the core of the city, this Gothic work of art is a demonstration of the expertise and art of ancient manufacturers. As you step inside, you can't resist the urge to feel a feeling of wonderment at the taking off curves, unpredictable carvings, and stained glass windows that embellish its corridors. However, Exeter's heritage isn't simply restricted to its house of prayer; it's woven into the texture of the whole city. From the old Roman walls that actually surround the downtown area to the archaic guildhalls that line the roads, tokens of Exeter's past are wherever you look.

Also, not disregarding individuals who have molded Exeter's legacy throughout the long term. From Roman warriors to middle age vendors, from Tudor aristocrats to Victorian industrialists, every age has transformed the city, adding to its rich and different woven artwork of societies and customs. Today, Exeter's legacy is commended and safeguarded by an enthusiastic local area of students of history, archeologists, and protectionists. Through their endeavors, we can proceed to explore and value the marvels of Exeter's past, guaranteeing that people in the future can encounter the sorcery of this noteworthy city for themselves.

So whether you're walking around the roads of the downtown area, exploring the remains of an old palace, or wondering about the excellence of a centuries-old basilica, pause for a minute to see the value in the rich heritage that encompasses you. It's an inheritance worth safeguarding, and a story worth imparting to the world.

3. EXETER TODAY

VIBRANT CULTURE AND CONTEMPORARY LIFE

Imagine yourself strolling down the clamoring roads of Exeter on a bright day, encompassed by the sights and hints of city life. Wherever you look, there's a buzz of energy from the energetic prattle of local people in walkway bistros to the giggling of kids playing in the parks.

However, Exeter's culture isn't just about what you see on a superficial level; about individuals calling this city home. Jump somewhat more profound, and you'll find a flourishing local area of specialists, performers, and creatives who mix Exeter with their energy and ability. Go for a walk through the downtown area and you'll find exhibitions displaying crafts by neighborhood specialists, theaters organizing enamoring exhibitions, and music scenes facilitating live gigs that will make them tap your feet and move along.

What's more? Considering the food scene. Exeter is a blend of culinary enjoyments, with eateries presenting everything from customary English passage to global cooking with a cutting edge turn. Whether you're longing for a good bar dinner, a fiery curry, or a connoisseur veggie lover feast, you'll track down everything here in Exeter.

However, maybe the most amazing aspect of Exeter's culture is its inclusivity and variety. Regardless of what your identity is or where you come from, you'll track down a warm greeting and a feeling of having a place around here. Whether you're going to a local area occasion, joining a neighborhood club, or basically starting up a discussion with a stranger, you'll before long find that Exeter is where everybody is gladly received.

EMBRACING TRADITION AMIDST MODERNITY

In the midst of Exeter ocean of custom, it is likewise a city that embraces the modern world with great enthusiasm. Step into the downtown area and you'll find smooth high rises hobnobbing with memorable structures, making a striking difference that catches the embodiment of Exeter's special person.

Explore and you'll find that practice and advancement are not in conflict; they coincide amicably, enhancing each other unexpectedly. From the customary business sectors that have been exchanging for a really long time to the inventive new companies that are molding the future, Exeter is a city where old and new meet up to make something genuinely unique.

Also, it's not simply in engineering and business that this mix of custom and advancement should be visible; it's woven into the texture of day to day existence. From the ceremonies and customs that have been gone down through ages to the state of the art innovation that controls our regular routines, Exeter is a city that praises its past while embracing the conceivable outcomes representing things to come.

So whether you explore the noteworthy milestones that speak the cityscape or test the most recent culinary manifestations at an in vogue eatery, pause for a minute to see the value in the wonderful embroidery of custom and advancement that makes Exeter the lively, unique city it is today.

PART 2: GETTING TO KNOW EXETER

4. PLANNING YOUR TRIP

PREPARING FOR YOUR EXETER ADVENTURE

Planning your experience in Exeter is the most important step towards creating enduring recollections in this dazzling city. Whether you're a first-time guest or returning to explore more, cautious readiness guarantees you capitalize on your time and experience all that Exeter brings to the table.

1. Research and Itinerary: Begin by investigating Exeter's attractions, occasions, and nearby culture. Make a schedule framing must-see tourist spots like Exeter Cathedral, the Royal Albert Memorial Museum, and the historic Quayside. Draw out time for comfortable strolls through the city's beguiling roads and investigate close by normal attractions like Dartmoor Public Park.

2. Convenience and Booking: Pick convenience that suits your inclinations and financial plan. Exeter offers a scope of choices from comfortable B&Bs in the downtown area to present day lodgings with riverside sees. Book your convenience ahead of time to get the best arrangements and guarantee an agreeable stay during your visit.

3. Pressing Essentials: Pack as indicated by the season and exercises arranged. Basics include happy strolling shoes for investigating cobblestone roads, climate suitable dress, sunscreen, and a reusable water bottle. Remember chargers for your gadgets and any important meds.

4. Transportation Plans: Settle on your favored method of transportation to Exeter; whether via train, vehicle, or transport; and organize appointments or rentals in like manner. If you aren't utilizing public vehicles inside the city, find out more about courses and timetables to explore effectively among attractions and neighborhoods.

5. Local Insights and Tips: Accumulate tips from fellow travelers or local people on hidden gems and eating proposals. Engaging with local people can give insider information on less popular attractions or impending occasions that could line up with your inclinations.

6. Safety and Health Considerations: Focus on safety by keeping crisis contact data and travel protection subtleties helpful. Look into nearby health administrations and rules if heading out during dubious times to guarantee a protected and pleasant excursion.

7. Embrace Flexibility: While planning is fundamental, stay adaptable to embrace surprising open doors or changes in your schedule. Pass on space for unconstrained disclosures and relaxed minutes to drench yourself in Exeter's appeal completely.

Planning for your Exeter experience makes way for an advancing and noteworthy experience. As you research, and do the necessary things needed to be done you can prepare to leave on an experience loaded up with social enjoyments, picturesque scenes, and warm neighborliness.

BEST TIMES TO VISIT EXETER

Picking the ideal opportunity to visit this enchanting city can upgrade your experience considerably more. The climate must be well considered and studied.

Exeter partakes in a gentle environment consistently, however if you favor hotter temperatures and clear skies, go for the gold throughout the mid-year months, from *June to August*. This is the point at which the city genuinely wakes up with outside occasions, celebrations, and clamoring markets, and also you'll have longer sunlight hours to take advantage of your touring experiences.

However, if you seriously love bright foliage and fresh fall air, **September to November** is an optimal opportunity to visit Exeter. The city's parks and gardens change into a shocking presentation of reds, oranges, and yellows, giving a pleasant setting to your investigations. Simply make certain to pack a few layers to remain comfortable as temperatures begin to plunge.

For the individuals who favor less groups and lower convenience costs, consider visiting during the shoulder times of **spring (Walk to March)** and *fall (September to November).* During these times, you'll appreciate the wonderful climate and a lot of attractions to investigate, however without the mid-year swarms.

Winter in Exeter can be similarly charming, particularly in the event that you love merry cheer. From late November through December, the city shimmers with occasion beautifications, Christmas markets, and occasional occasions. It's the ideal chance to taste reflected on wine, search for remarkable gifts, and absorb the comfortable air.

So the best chance to visit Exeter relies upon your own inclinations and interests. Whether you're looking for daylight filled days or bubbly occasion flows, this enchanting city brings something to the table for all year. So go on, plan your excursion, and prepare to make extraordinary recollections in Exeter!

5. GETTING TO EXETER

NAVIGATING TRANSPORTATION OPTIONS

Getting to Exeter ought to be all around as energizing as investigating the actual city. Whether you're a neighbor arranging a road trip or a guest from a far distance, picking the right transportation choice can have a significant effect by the way you start your experience.

Via Train

Taking the train to Exeter isn't simply an excursion; it's a beautiful encounter. Trains associate Exeter to significant urban areas like London, Bristol, and Birmingham effortlessly. You can sit back, unwind, and partake in the wide open perspectives as you head towards Exeter St Davids station, the primary rail line center. Trains offer solace and comfort, particularly for the individuals who lean toward trying not to traffic and partake in a problem complementary lift.

Via Car

Heading to Exeter gives you the opportunity to investigate at your own speed. Significant motorways like the M5 give direct courses into the city from different pieces of the UK. It's an incredible choice in the event that you need adaptability, permitting you to stop at beguiling towns or picturesque spots en route. Make a point to check traffic updates and plan your course to stay away from delays, guaranteeing a smooth drive.

By Bus

For frugal explorers, transports offer a solid and practical method for arriving at Exeter. Public and local transport administrations work incessant courses associating Exeter to local towns and urban areas. It's a helpful decision on the off chance that you favor another person to do the driving while you unwind and partake in the excursion. Transports frequently have numerous quits, making them available from numerous areas.

Getting ready for Your Adventure

Beyond setting off on your excursion to Exeter, think about these fundamental arrangements:

- *Tickets and Reservations*: Whether you're reserving train tickets, saving a rental vehicle, or buying transport tickets, it's fundamental to have your itinerary items affirmed ahead of time. This evades last-minute pressure and guarantees you grab a chair saved.

- *Climate Awareness*: Really look at the weather conditions conjecture for

Exeter prior to pressing. Bring fitting apparel and embellishments, for example, an umbrella or sunscreen relying upon the season to remain agreeable all through your excursion.

- ***Nearby Insights***: Explore neighborhood attractions, eating choices, and any occasions or celebrations occurring during your visit. Along these lines, you can design your agenda and take full advantage of your time in Exeter, finding both well known milestones and unlikely treasures.

- ***Solace Essentials***: Pack fundamentals for your excursion, for example, snacks, a reusable water bottle, diversion like books or music, and any prescriptions you might require. These things guarantee you stay agreeable and ready during movement.

Exploring transportation choices to Exeter is about something other than arriving at an objective, it's tied in with partaking in the excursion and capitalizing on your movement experience. Gather your packs, plan your course, and prepare to set out on an essential experience in Exeter, where each excursion starts with expectation and finishes with remarkable encounters.

TIPS FOR HASSLE-FREE TRAVEL TO EXETER

Making a trip to Exeter ought to be the beginning of an intriguing experience, not a wellspring of stress. These functional tips will guarantee your excursion to Exeter is smooth and charming.

- Plan Ahead

Arranging is critical to a problem free outing. Research your transportation choices; whether it's via train, vehicle, or transport; and pick the choice that best suits your inclinations and spending plan. Book your tickets or reserve a spot ahead of time to get your seats and stay away from last-minute rush.

- Really take a look at Movement Updates

Remain refreshed on tourism warnings and course data. Check for any disturbances or postpones that might influence your excursion, particularly assuming you're going during busy times or unfriendly weather patterns. Being educated permits you to design elective courses if important.

- Pack Light and Smart

Pressing effectively can have a major effect. Bring fundamentals like happiness with dress, climate proper stuff, and any meds you might require. Consider the exercises you have arranged in Exeter to pack appropriately, yet attempt to keep your baggage sensible for more straightforward versatility.

- Remain Organized
Keep all your movement archives, tickets, and distinguishing proof effectively available. This incorporates your visa (if voyaging universally), train or transport tickets, convenience subtleties, and any affirmations. Sorting out these things in advance saves time and diminishes pressure during registrations and moves.

- Embrace Flexibility
Travel can now and again accompany unforeseen amazements. Remain adaptable and patient in the event that

things don't go precisely as expected. Have a contingency plan for convenience or exercises in the event of changes, and keep an uplifting perspective to capitalize on your experience.

- **Investigate Nearby Insights**

Before you show up, get to know Exeter's attractions, feasting choices, and nearby culture. Research well known milestones, unlikely treasures, and occasions occurring during your visit. This information upgrades your excursion as well as assists you explore the city with certainty.

- **Partake in the Journey**

Recall that movement isn't just about arriving at your objective, it's about the encounters en route. Whether you're partaking in the landscape on a train ride, investigating new spots via vehicle, or meeting individual voyagers on a transport, embrace every snapshot of your excursion to Exeter.

Following these tips will guarantee your movement to Exeter, smooth and tranquil as could be expected.

6. GETTING AROUND EXETER

EXPLORING THE CITY'S LAYOUT

Exploring a city like Exeter can be both invigorating and a piece overwhelming. Understanding the layout of Exeter won't just assist you with getting around proficiently yet in addition permit you to take advantage of your time exploring its charms.

The Core Of Exeter

Exeter's downtown area is where a large part of the activity occurs. Here you'll find notable milestones like Exeter Basilica, Guildhall Mall, and the Illustrious Albert Dedication Historical center. The middle is smaller and walkable, making it ideal for investigating by walking. Meander through limited middle age roads fixed with shops, bistros, and cafés, absorbing the city's rich history and dynamic air.

Quayside and Waterway Exe
Toward the south of the downtown area lies Exeter Quayside, a beautiful region along the Waterway Exe. This waterfront area offers picturesque strolls, waterside feasting, and relaxation exercises. Investigate the noteworthy Exeter Quay with its second hand stores, shops and bars housed in old distribution centers, or go on a loosening up boat outing along the stream to appreciate perspectives on the city according to an alternate point of view.

College and West Exeter
Traveling northwards, you'll track down the College of Exeter grounds and the vivacious neighborhood of St. David's. This region is known for its understudy

accommodating energy, mixed bistros, and social settings like the Exeter Northcott Theater. West Exeter expands further into neighborhoods and green spaces, offering a calmer side of the city away from the clamoring place.

External Locale and Beyond

Exeter's layout stretches out into different external regions, each with its own exceptional person. From rural neighborhoods to provincial edges, these regions offer a blend of private living, nearby conveniences, and regular scenes. Whether you're investigating Heavitree with its town-like feel or wandering into the encompassing open country, there's a lot to find past the downtown area.

Tips for Exploring:
- ***Strolling and Cycling***: Exeter is person on foot cordial, with numerous ways and cycle courses for investigating

both the city and its edges. Leasing a bicycle or essentially walking around permits you to see the value in the city's design and unlikely treasures at your own speed.

- **Public Transport**: For longer excursions or investigating external areas, Exeter offers dependable transport administrations interfacing different pieces of the city. Actually look at courses and plans in advance to take full advantage of your movements.

- **Nearby Insight**: Draw in with local people and request suggestions. They frequently know the best spots to visit, whether it's a comfortable bistro, a grand perspective, or a less popular verifiable site.

Understanding Exeter's layout makes investigating the city a superb encounter.

From the dynamic downtown area to the quiet riverside and then some, every region offers its own appeal and potential open doors for disclosure. Thus, snatch a guide, trim up your strolling shoes, and prepare to reveal the excellence and variety of Exeter in each area in turn.

TRANSPORTATION WITHIN EXETER

Getting around Exeter is a breeze with its helpful transportation choices custom-made for local people and guests the same. Whether you incline toward strolling through memorable roads or bouncing on open vehicles, investigating the city has never been simpler.

1. Walking: One of the most amazing ways of encountering Exeter is walking.

The downtown area is conservative and person on foot agreeable, making it ideal for comfortable walks. Meander through tight paths fixed with shops, bistros, and verifiable milestones like Exeter Church building. Strolling not just permits you to absorb the city's climate yet additionally gives you the opportunity to find unlikely treasures concealed in corners.

2. Cycling: For the individuals who appreciate cycling, Exeter offers assigned bicycle paths and ways that confuse the city and its edges. Lease a bicycle from one of the nearby shops or bring your own to investigate further abroad. Cycling is a fast and eco-accommodating method for getting around, permitting you to make more progress while partaking in the outside air and picturesque perspectives along the Stream Exe or through green parks.

3. Transport Services: Exeter flaunts a solid transport network worked by Stagecoach and other nearby suppliers. Transports associate the downtown area with encompassing areas, rural areas, and attractions. Whether you're going to the College of Exeter grounds, the notable Quayside, or shopping at Guildhall Retail outlet, there's a reasonable transport course that meets your requirements. Check timetables and courses in advance or utilize portable applications for constant updates to proficiently design your excursion.

4. Cabs and Ride-Sharing: At the point when you really want a fast and helpful ride, cabs and ride-sharing administrations are promptly accessible in Exeter. They give house to house transport, ideal for voyaging late around evening time or when you have weighty gear. Taxicabs can be flagged down in the city or booked ahead of time through nearby organizations or versatile applications.

Ways to get Around:
- *City Maps*: Get a city map from traveler data focuses or download a computerized guide to effortlessly explore Exeter's roads and milestones.

- *Parking*: Assuming you're driving, know about stopping zones and offices around the city. Consider utilizing park-and-ride administrations situated on the edges for problem free admittance to the downtown area.

- *Strolling Tours*: Join directed strolling visits to find out about Exeter's set of experiences, design, and neighborhood legends from educated guides who rejuvenate the city's accounts.

Exploring transportation inside Exeter is direct and upgrades your experience of this enchanting city. Whether you favor the opportunity of strolling, the speed of cycling, or the comfort of public vehicles, there's a method of transportation to suit each voyager's inclination.

PART 3: EXPERIENCING EXETER

7. LANDMARKS AND ATTRACTIONS

MUST-SEE SIGHTS IN EXETER

Exeter is a city overflowing with history, culture, and normal excellence, offering guests a mother lode of must-see locates that catch its embodiment. Whether you're a set of experiences buff, a nature lover, or basically looking for essential encounters, these milestones and attractions are not to be missed during your visit.

Exeter Cathedral

A transcending work of art of Gothic design, Exeter Cathedral is the highlight of the city's horizon. Step inside to wonder about its taking off vaulted roofs, unpredictable stained glass windows, and the longest continuous archaic stone vault on the planet. Try not to miss the rooftop visit for all encompassing perspectives on Exeter and then some.

Royal Albert Memorial Museum (RAMM)

Submerge yourself in workmanship, culture, and history at RAMM, a Victorian-period historical center that houses a different assortment of relics spreading over hundreds of years. From Egyptian mummies to neighborhood archeological searches, each show recounts an account of Exeter's rich legacy and worldwide associations.

Exeter Quayside

Walk around the pleasant Exeter Quayside, where noteworthy distribution centers have been changed into popular bistros, bars, and stores. Watch boats tenderly weaving on the Waterway Exe, eat in the open air with waterfront perspectives, or go on a comfortable boat outing to investigate the city according to an alternate point of view.

Underground Passages
Dive into Exeter's middle age past with a directed visit through the Underground

passages. Inherent in the 14th century to supply water to the city, these sections offer an interesting look into day to day existence hundreds of years prior. Find out about the difficulties of keeping up with these perplexing passages and envision life in archaic Exeter.

Northernhay Gardens

Get away from the rushing about of the city in Northernhay Nurseries, perhaps Britain's most seasoned public nursery. Meander through finished yards, botanical presentations, and serene pathways fixed with noteworthy sculptures and landmarks. It's the ideal spot for a serene evening outing or a comfortable walk around plant life.

Red Coat Guided Tours

Join a Red Coat Directed Visit to uncover Exeter's surprise, yet invaluable treasures and stories with proficient neighborhood guides. Browse themed visits like the City Wall Trail, Phantoms and Legends, or House of God to Mausoleums, each offering special bits of knowledge into Exeter's interesting history and lively culture.

Dartmoor National Park

Adventure is simply a short drive from Exeter to investigate the rough magnificence of Dartmoor National Park. Home to emotional scenes, antiquated stone circles, and meandering Dartmoor horses, this regular jungle gym offers vast open doors for climbing, cycling, or basically absorbing amazing perspectives.

Investigating these high priority sights in Exeter guarantees an excursion through time, culture, and regular magnificence. Exeter welcomes you to submerge yourself in its appeal and make extraordinary recollections. From famous milestones to unlikely treasures, each sight recounts an account of Exeter's over a significant time span, ready to be found and esteemed during your visit.

HIDDEN GEMS WAITING TO BE DISCOVERED

While Exeter is known for its famous tourist spots, there are a lot of hidden gems dispersed all through the city that offer extraordinary and vital encounters. These less popular spots permit you to reveal the rich history, culture, and appeal of Exeter past the standard vacation destinations.

1. Mol's Espresso House: Mol's Café is an interesting jewel tracing all the way back to the sixteenth hundred years. Step inside this notable structure to partake in some espresso or tea in the midst of comfortable environmental elements enhanced with one of a kind stylistic layout. It's an ideal spot to unwind and absorb the climate of old-world Exeter.

2. Exhausts Hall: Find Exhausts Corridor, an unlikely treasure wrapped behind High Road up the core of Exeter. This notable guildhall traces all the way back to the fifteenth hundred years and offers a brief look into the city's exchanging past. Appreciate the unpredictable woodwork and finished glass windows as you find out about Exeter's dealers and their organization customs.

3. St. Martin's Church:

Get away from the clamoring downtown area and visit St. Martin's Church, concealed in a tranquil corner close to the Guildhall Mall. This middle age church flaunts a quiet environment and staggering stained glass windows, making it a peaceful safe-haven in the midst of the metropolitan scene.

4. Parliament Street:

Explore Parliament street, one of Exeter's secret compositional wonders.

This thin path professes to be the world's tightest road for vehicles, with houses inclining towards one another at the upper floors, making a novel and enchanting air. Meander through this notable path to encounter a cut of old-world appeal.

5. Exeter's Archaic City Wall: Go for a walk along Exeter's middle age city wall, which once shielded the city from intruders. Portions of the wall are as yet flawless close to Northernhay Nurseries and Rougemont Palace, offering a brief look into Exeter's invigorated past. Stroll along these old fortresses and envision the city's authentic guards.

6. Gandy Street:

Investigate Gandy Road, an unexpected, yet invaluable treasure fixed with free shops, bistros, and exhibitions. This beautiful road traces all the way back to the fourteenth hundred years and radiates a bohemian enchant with its cobblestones and peculiar customer facing facades. Find one of a kind keepsakes, distinctive products, and nearby craftsmanship as you meander through this lively area.

7. The House that Moved: Wonder about the House that Moved, an engineering wonder tucked in the midst of Exeter's advanced roads. The fourteenth century forest outlined house was moved during the 1960s to clear a path for street extension, saving a piece of Exeter's set of experiences and exhibiting the city's commitment to preservation and legacy.

Embrace the experience of finding these nearby fortunes and allow them to advance your experience of this charming city.

8. CULTURAL EXPERIENCES

DIVING INTO EXETER'S CULTURAL SCENE

Exeter's culture scene is an embroidery woven with history, innovativeness, and local area soul. Whether you're a set of experienced lovers, craftsmanship enthusiast, or just interested about nearby customs, plunging into Exeter's social scene guarantees a rich and vivid experience that uncovers the city's spirit.

- **Historical centers and Galleries**

Drench yourself in Exeter's imaginative legacy at the Royal Albert Remembrance Memorial Museum (RAMM), where old antiquities, intuitive displays, and contemporary craftsmanship assortments rejuvenate history.

Investigate exhibitions displaying everything from neighborhood Devonshire fortunes to worldwide archeological finds, giving experiences into Exeter's over a significant time span.

- **Theaters and Performances**

Experience the enchantment of live exhibitions at Exeter's theaters, like the Exeter Phoenix and the Northcott Theater. From state of the art plays and melodic exhibitions to provocative workmanship establishments, these scenes have a different scope of far-reaching developments that praise inventiveness and development.

- **Music and Festivals**

Observe Exeter's dynamic music scene at celebrations like the Exeter Celebration of South West Food and Drink, where neighborhood performers, gourmet specialists, and craftsmans meet up to feature their gifts. From customary society music to contemporary beats, these occasions offer a sample of Exeter's social variety and local area soul.

- **Authentic Landmarks**

Step back in time as you investigate Exeter's authentic tourist spots, like the overwhelming Exeter Basilica and the archaic Guildhall. Directed visits offer bits of knowledge into compositional wonders and the accounts they hold, uncovering how the city has developed over hundreds of years while saving its legacy.

- **Neighborhood Customs and Events**

Draw in with Exeter's neighborhood customs and occasions, for example, the Exeter Christmas Market or the Exeter Pride March. These local meetings praise variety, innovativeness, and inclusivity, mirroring the city's inviting soul and dynamic social embroidered artwork.

- **Culinary Experiences**

Find Exeter's culinary joys through food celebrations, ranchers' business sectors, and high quality food visits. From conventional Devonshire cream teas to imaginative eating encounters, Exeter's culinary scene mixes neighborhood flavors with worldwide impacts, offering a blowout for the faculties.

- **Inventive Studios and Classes**

Take part in imaginative studios and classes presented by nearby specialists and skilled workers. Whether you're keen on stoneware, painting, or photography, these involved encounters permit you to release your imagination while gaining from skilled experts in a steady climate.

Plunging into Exeter's social scene is something beyond investigating galleries and going to exhibitions; it's tied in with associating with the city's set of experiences, embracing imagination, and commending the local area. Embrace the amazing chance to dive into Exeter's social embroidery and find the tales that shape this lively city.

IMMERSING YOURSELF IN LOCAL TRADITIONS

Exeter offers an abundance of local traditions ready to be found. Embracing these practices permits you to associate profoundly with the substance of the city, encountering firsthand the traditions and values that have molded Exeter's character over hundreds of years.

- ***Embrace the Bubbly Spirit***:
Participate in the merriments during occasional occasions, for example, the Exeter Christmas Market or the Exeter Pride March. These festivals unite local people and guests the same to respect customs, share euphoria, and celebrate variety. From bright processions to happy business sectors, these occasions feature Exeter's lively local area soul.

- ***Find Culinary Delights***:
Taste the kinds of Exeter through its culinary practices. Enjoy a Devonshire cream tea with newly heated scones and coagulated cream, or relish nearby claims to fame at ranchers' business sectors and food celebrations. From conventional recipes gone down through ages to imaginative feasting encounters, Exeter's food culture mirrors its rich agrarian legacy and beach front abundance.

- *Investigate Noteworthy Customs*:

Dig into Exeter's set of experiences by investigating its noteworthy traditions and practices. Visit the Guildhall to find out about old urban functions and customs that keep on being noticed today. From organization customs to formal occasions, these practices give experiences into Exeter's administration and local area life all through the ages.

- *Participate in Expressions and Crafts*:

Partake in studios and classes that observe Exeter's creative customs. Learn stoneware methods motivated by nearby dirt stores, or join painting classes that draw motivation from the city's scenes and engineering. These involved encounters interface you with nearby craftsmans and specialists, protecting and passing on customary abilities.

- **_Go to Social Festivals_**:

Submerge yourself in Exeter's social variety by going to celebrations that feature music, dance, and craftsmanship from around the world. From people's celebrations celebrating customary music to multicultural occasions featuring worldwide cooking and customs, these celebrations cultivate multifaceted comprehension and appreciation inside the local area.

- **_Visit Memorable Sites_**:

Investigate Exeter's memorable destinations and milestones where customs have been safeguarded and regarded for ages. Visit the Exeter House of Prayer to observe exceptionally old customs and strict practices, or visit St. Nicholas Cloister to find out about day to day existence in middle age Exeter. These destinations offer looks into the city's past and the practices that have molded its social scene.

- **_Support Neighborhood Craftsmans and Businesses:_**
Shop locally to help craftsmans and organizations that maintain Exeter's practices and craftsmanship. Buy high quality merchandise at craftsman markets or peruse store shops offering privately obtained items. By putting resources into nearby craftsmanship and innovativeness, you add to the protection and advancement of Exeter's social legacy.

Drenching yourself in Exeter's neighborhood customs is an excursion of revelation, association, and festivity. Embrace the chance to partake in and protect these customs, guaranteeing they proceed to flourish and rouse people in the future in this notable city.

9. OUTDOOR ADVENTURES

NATURE ESCAPES IN AND AROUND EXETER

Exeter isn't just about its notable appeal and clamoring city life; it likewise offers nature lovers plenty of open air getaways to investigate and appreciate. These regular marvels around Exeter guarantee extraordinary encounters in nature.

1. Dartmoor National Park:

Simply a short drive from Exeter lies Dartmoor National Park, a rambling wild of rough moorland, old forests, and transcending stone peaks. Ribbon up your climbing boots and set out on picturesque paths that breeze through heather-clad slopes, close by quiet waterways, and past enchanted stone circles. Watch out for Dartmoor's famous horses touching uninhibitedly across the scene.

2. Haldon Forest Park:

Nearer to the city, Haldon Forest Park offers a sanctuary for outside fans, everything being equal. Investigate miles of strolling, cycling, and pony riding trails that breeze through coniferous forests and open heathland. Challenge yourself on the elating Flip out treetop experience course or partake in a relaxed cookout in the midst of serene environmental factors.

3. River Exe and Exeter Canal:

Find the regular excellence along the Waterway Exe and Exeter Canal, where picturesque boat trips, kayaking outings, and riverside strolls anticipate. Watch for natural life like herons, kingfishers, and otters along the streams, or essentially loosen up on the keeps money with an excursion while absorbing peaceful perspectives.

4. Exe Estuary Trail:

Cycle or walk the Exe Estuary Trail, a pleasant course that stretches from Exeter to the beachfront towns of Exmouth and Dawlish. Follow level, sans traffic ways along the estuary, going through nature saves overflowing with birdlife and offering looks at Devon's shocking shoreline.

5. Powderham Castle and Deer Park:

Investigate the grounds of Powderham Palace and its sweeping Deer Park, where memorable nurseries, forest strolls, and beautiful perspectives over the Exe Estuary anticipate. Meander through antiquated trees, spot brushing deer, and visit the walled nursery to appreciate occasional sprouts and exceptionally old engineering.

6. Beaches and Coastal Walks: Getaway to Exeter's close by sea shores and beach front strolls for an invigorating coastline retreat. Go to local objections like Exmouth or Teignmouth to walk around sandy shores, appreciate frozen yogurt on the wharf, or take a dunk in the reviving waters of the English Channel.

7. Nature Reserves and Gardens: Find Exeter's secret normal diamonds inside nearby nature holds and gardens. Visit places like the Devon Natural life Trust's Cricklepit Factory, where wetlands and bird stows away give asylum to nearby natural life. Investigate professional flowerbeds like Killerton House and Gardens, with its staggering arranged grounds and occasional botanical presentations.

Nature escapes in and around Exeter offer an ideal equilibrium to city life, furnishing open doors to reconnect with nature, loosen up in serene environmental factors, and investigate different scenes.

THRILLING OUTDOOR ACTIVITIES FOR EVERY ADVENTURER

Exeter is likewise a jungle gym for outside devotees looking for exciting experiences in nature. Whether you're a thrill seeker or just hoping to have a go at a new thing, these outdoor exercises around Exeter guarantee fervor, picturesque perspectives, and remarkable encounters in nature.

***1. Coasteering along the Jurassic Coast*:**

Leave on an outright exhilarating coasteering experience along the dazzling Jurassic Coast close to Exeter. Tie on a wetsuit and head protector as you explore rough bluffs, swim through regular ocean caverns, and jump into completely clear waters. Directed visits take care of all expertise levels, guaranteeing a protected and elating experience investigating Devon's tough shore.

2. Climbing and Bouldering at Dartmoor:

Challenge yourself with rock climbing and bouldering experiences in the midst of Dartmoor National Park's emotional stone pinnacles. Whether you're a carefully prepared climber or a novice, Dartmoor offers different courses and stunning perspectives that make each rising fulfilling. Join directed meetings to learn strategies and find stowed away climbing spots.

3. Kayaking on the River Exe:

Paddle along the peaceful waters of the Stream Exe, encompassed by pleasant open country and plentiful untamed life. Lease a kayak or join a directed visit to investigate stowed away brooks, spot herons and otters, and appreciate all encompassing perspectives on Exeter's riverside magnificence. Kayaking is reasonable for all ages and expertise levels, making it an ideal family-accommodating experience.

4. *Mountain Biking at Haldon Forest Park:*
Raise a ruckus around town at Haldon Forest Park for an elating mountain trekking experience through forest tracks and testing landscape. With trails going from simple to cutting edge, cyclists, everything being equal, can appreciate exciting drops, specialized climbs, and all encompassing perspectives across the Devonshire open country.

5. *Horseback Riding on Dartmoor:*
Investigate Dartmoor's wild scenes riding a horse, riding through old forests, heather-covered slopes, and open moorland. Directed horse riding visits offer an exceptional viewpoint on Dartmoor's regular magnificence and

social legacy, permitting you to interface with the scene and its occupant horses.

6. Zip-Lining at Go Ape, Haldon Forest:

Take off through the treetops on a zip-lining experience at Flip out, Haldon Backwoods. Explore high ropes courses, swing across impediments, and zip-line through the shade for an adrenaline-sipping experience encompassed by staggering timberland landscape. Reasonable for daredevils, all things considered, Fly off the handle offers a thrilling outside challenge in a protected and controlled climate.

7. Stand-Up Paddleboarding (SUP) on Exeter's Canals:

Attempt stand-up paddleboarding (SUP) on Exeter's serene trenches, ideal for amateurs and prepared paddlers the same. Skim along the streams, absorbing city perspectives and untamed life sightings according to a one of a kind point of view. SUP examples and rentals are accessible, making it an unwinding yet daring method for investigating Exeter's metropolitan and regular scenes.

From coasteering along rough precipices to zip-lining through woodland overhangs, Exeter offers exciting outside exercises that take special care of each and every swashbuckler. Whether you're looking for adrenaline-siphoning difficulties or quiet nature encounters, these exercises welcome you to investigate Devon's assorted scenes and make enduring recollections in nature. Pack your feeling of experience and find the reason why Exeter is the final location for outside devotees of any age and interests.

PART 4: LIVING IN EXETER

10. ACCOMMODATION OPTIONS

FINDING YOUR HOME AWAY FROM HOME

Envision venturing into a spot that immediately feels like it was made only for you. Some place that encloses you by solace, greets you wholeheartedly, and turns into your safe-haven away from the hurrying around of daily existence. That is the wizardry of viewing as your usual hangout spot in Exeter.

Investigating Your Options

Exeter, with its interesting appeal and dynamic local area, offers an assortment of convenience choices custom fitted to suit each need and inclination. Whether you're an understudy leaving on another scholastic excursion, an expert looking for a quiet retreat, or a family hoping to get comfortable in a well disposed area, Exeter has something extraordinary sitting tight for you.

Understudy Well disposed Spaces

For understudies, finding a spot that upholds both scholastic pursuits and self-awareness is critical. Envision residing in a comfortable understudy home where companionships are fashioned over late-night concentrate on meetings and shared chuckling. These spaces offer comfort as well as encourage a feeling of having a place inside a unique understudy local area.

Solaces of Home

If you're looking for a more long-lasting home, Exeter's areas offer a different exhibit of homes and condos. Imagine yourself in an enchanting condo with a nursery where you can loosen up following a bustling day, or in a cutting edge loft with all encompassing perspectives on the city horizon. Every choice gives the solaces of home while permitting you to investigate all that Exeter brings to the table.

Local area and Connection
 Past a spot to reside, seeing as your usual hangout spot in Exeter implies turning out to be important for a warm and inviting local area. Whether it's visiting with neighbors over some tea, finding unlikely treasures in the nearby business sectors, or joining local area occasions and celebrations, you'll find that Exeter embraces everybody with great affection.

Making It Your Own
 The excellence of viewing as your usual hangout spot lies in the opportunity to make it your own. From enriching your space with individual contacts to

investigating the city's social contributions, Exeter urges you to make recollections that will endure forever. Whether you favor the tranquil quietness of a rustic retreat or the energetic buzz of city living, Exeter's convenience choices take care of different preferences and ways of life.

Viewing as your usual hangout spot in Exeter isn't just about picking a spot to reside; it's tied in with finding where you should be. With its rich history, cordial environment, and vast open doors for experience, Exeter invites you to set out on an excursion of revelation and make a daily existence that feels genuinely yours.

ACCOMMODATION CHOICES FOR EVERY BUDGET

Finding the perfect place to stay isn't just about finding a roof over your head; it's about discovering a space that feels like it was made just for you. In Exeter, whether you're on a shoestring budget or looking to splurge, there's a place that fits your needs and feels like home.

Budget-Friendly Options
1. *St. Andrews Hotel -*

This charming bed and breakfast provides cozy rooms at reasonable rates, ideal for those seeking a homely atmosphere without breaking the bank.

Mid-Range Comfort
1. *Jurys Inn Exeter* -With modern amenities and a central location, Jurys Inn Exeter caters to travelers looking for comfort without exceeding their budget.

2. *The Devon Hotel* -

Known for its warm hospitality and spacious rooms, The Devon Hotel is a popular choice among visitors seeking mid-range accommodation with a touch of luxury.

3. Mercure Exeter Rougemont Hotel -Set in a historic building, this hotel combines classic elegance with contemporary comforts, offering a tranquil retreat in the heart of the city.

Luxurious Retreats
1. Southernhay House Hotel -

For those seeking a boutique experience, Southernhay House Hotel offers luxury rooms and personalized service in a historic Georgian townhouse.

2. *Hotel du Vin Exeter* -

Housed in a former eye hospital, this upscale hotel features stylish rooms, a renowned bistro, and a relaxing spa, perfect for indulging in a luxurious stay.

3. *Lympstone Manor Hotel* -Located just outside Exeter, this five-star country house hotel offers stunning views,

gourmet dining, and bespoke service for a truly unforgettable escape.

These are a few hotels to take for a lodge. Others includes: Courtyard Exeter Sandy Park, Mercure Exeter Rougemont hotel, Travelodge Exeter M5, Globe Backpackers, City gate, Bendene Town house, Telstar Hotel, Toby Hotel, Cedar Lodge Hotel and many more.

No matter your budget or preference, Exeter offers a range of accommodation choices that feel like a home away from home. So, pack your bags, choose your perfect retreat, and let Exeter welcome you with open arms to your new home away from home.

11. DINING AND SHOPPING

SAVORY DELIGHTS AND CULINARY JOURNEYS

Envision a city where each feast is an excursion of flavors, where each chomp recounts an account of custom, development, and neighborhood pride. Welcome to Exeter, where feasting isn't just about eating, about setting out on a culinary experience tempts your taste buds and leaves you hankering more.

Neighborhood Jewels and Secret Treasures

In Exeter, you'll find plenty of feasting choices that take care of each and every sense of taste and inclination. From curious bistros concealed in enchanting rear entryways to clamoring eateries along the high road, every foundation offers a one of a kind feasting experience that mirrors the city's rich social embroidery.

Conventional Charge with a Twist

For those hankering conventional English cooking with a cutting edge turn, Exeter's gastro pubs and restaurants present good works of art like fried fish and French fries, Devonshire cream teas, and privately obtained meats and cheeses. Envision relishing an impeccably cooked Sunday dish or enjoying a wanton evening tea in the midst of comfortable environmental elements that vibe like home.

Worldwide Flavors, Nearby Ingredients

Exeter's culinary scene likewise brags a different cluster worldwide flavors, impacted by worldwide cooking styles and utilizing new, privately obtained fixings. Whether you're in the mood for credible Italian pasta, zesty Indian curries, fragrant

Thai dishes, or flavorful French luxuries, you'll find everything reachable.

Ranchers' Business sectors and Foodie Havens

Past eateries, Exeter's dynamic food culture reaches out to its clamoring ranchers' business sectors and distinctive food shops. Picture walking around slows down overflowing with newly prepared bread, artisan cheeses, natural produce, and handcrafted chocolates, all created with care and energy by nearby makers.

Culinary Encounters to Remember

For those hoping to raise their feasting experience, Exeter offers culinary studios, food visits, and tasting occasions that permit you to submerge yourself in the city's gastronomic pleasures. Whether you're figuring out how to prepare conventional scones, testing nearby wines, or investigating the privileged insights of cheddar making, these encounters make certain to have an enduring effect.

Eating isn't simply a need; it's a necessary area of the city's way of life and personality. Whether you're a food fan, an inquisitive voyager, or nearby hoping to investigate new flavors, Exeter welcomes you to leave on an exquisite excursion that commends the specialty of food and the delight of shared dinners. Along these lines, come hungry, investigate energetically, and let Exeter's culinary miracles enchant your faculties and sustain your spirit.

SHOPPING EXPERIENCES IN EXETER

Picture strolling down cobbled streets lined with quaint shops and bustling market stalls, the air filled with excitement and anticipation. Exeter is a place where shopping isn't just about buying things, it's about uncovering treasures, exploring local craftsmanship, and indulging in a bit of retail therapy that's uniquely satisfying.

Charming Boutiques and Unique Finds

Exeter boasts a charming array of independent boutiques and specialty shops that cater to every taste and style. Whether you're searching for handmade jewelry, vintage clothing, artisanal crafts, or bespoke gifts, you'll find hidden gems tucked away in every corner of the city.

High Street Delights

For those who prefer the convenience of familiar brands and department stores, Exeter's bustling high street offers a mix of well-known retailers alongside local favorites. From fashion and accessories to homeware and electronics, the high street promises a shopping experience that combines variety with accessibility.

Market Magic

No visit to Exeter is complete without exploring its vibrant markets, where the hustle and bustle of traders and the aroma of freshly cooked street food create an atmosphere of lively energy. Whether you're browsing for fresh produce, handmade treats, or unique souvenirs, the markets provide a sensory feast that celebrates local flavors and craftsmanship.

Retail Therapy with a View

Imagine shopping with a view, Exeter's Princesshay shopping center offers just that, with its modern architecture and open-air design complementing a diverse selection of shops and restaurants. Here, you can shop to your heart's content while enjoying panoramic views of the city skyline and the historic cathedral.

Hidden Corners and Local Artisans
 Beyond the main shopping areas, Exeter invites exploration of its hidden corners and alleyways, where independent artisans and creatives showcase their talents in quaint studios and workshops. Discover handcrafted pottery, bespoke leather goods, intricate artwork, and more, all crafted with passion and precision.

 Shopping in Exeter is about immersing yourself in the city's vibrant culture, supporting local businesses, and finding joy in the art of discovery. Exeter offers shopping experiences that are as enriching as they are enjoyable. So, grab your shopping bags, explore at your own pace, and let Exeter surprise you with its delightful array of shopping treasures waiting to be uncovered.

PART 5:
EXPLORING
BEYOND EXETER

12. DAY TRIPS AND EXCURSIONS

VENTURING BEYOND THE CITY LIMITS

At times, the best undertakings lie just past the recognizable cityscape. Exeter offers a door to a universe of revelation and unwinding. Whether you're wanting nature's serenity, verifiable wonders, or basically a difference in view, wandering past as far as possible commitments extraordinary encounters.

Embracing Nature's Beauty

Envision exchanging high rises for clearing scenes and city commotion for the relieving hints of nature. Simply a short drive from Exeter, Devon's wide open unfurls like an intricate interwoven pattern of green fields and winding paths. Investigate Dartmoor's rough peaks, where wild horses meander uninhibitedly, or Dartmoor Public Park's pleasant towns, where time appears to stop. Each side of the wide open welcomes you to inhale profoundly, re-energize, and associate with the earth.

Waterfront Charms

For those captivated by the ocean, Devon's shoreline coaxes with its sandy shores, sensational precipices, and enchanting coastline towns. Imagine yourself walking around the promenade at Exmouth, tasting newly got fried fish and French fries at Sidmouth, or watching the waves run into the stones at Dawlish. Whether you're looking for sun-doused unwinding or strengthening waterfront strolls, the seashores and towns close to Exeter offer a reviving departure.

Venture Through History

History buffs will take pleasure in Devon's rich woven artwork of legacy locales and old tourist spots. Step back in time as you meander through the Roman remnants at Exeter's Underground Sections or investigate the superb Powderham Palace, settled along the Waterway Exe. Each site recounts an account of bygone ages, offering bits of knowledge into Devon's celebrated past and structural wonders that keep on motivating stunningness.

Family Adventures

Arranging a family day out? Devon's trips from Exeter take care of any age with an abundance of exercises. Visit natural life parks like Paignton Zoo, where fascinating creatures wander in the midst of rich vegetation, or leave on a nostalgic excursion on board a steam train at the South Devon Rail line. Intuitive galleries, experience stops, and cultivated attractions guarantee that each individual from the family can make appreciated recollections together.

Culinary Delights

Exploring beyond Exeter additionally implies enjoying Devon's culinary fortunes. From ranch-to-table feasting encounters to curious lunch nooks serving newly heated scones, Devon's gastronomic scene celebrates neighborhood flavors and fixings. Leave on a foodie trail through Devon's open country, examining craftsman cheeses, tasting on juice at customary plantations, and finding the insider facts of Devonshire cream teas.

Venturing beyond the city furthest reaches of Exeter opens a universe of potential outcomes, where nature's magnificence, history's charm, and culinary joys anticipate. Pack your feeling of wonder, set out in a less common direction, and let Devon's captivating scenes and social fortunes enhance your next escape from city life.

UNVEILING EXETER'S SURROUNDING WONDERS

Get away from the city buzz of Exeter and find the amazing fortunes that lie just past its lines. You may be nearby looking for new undertakings or a guest anxious to explore, Exeter's environmental elements offer an embroidery of regular excellence, captivating history, and extraordinary encounters.

Dartmoor National Park

Simply a short drive from Exeter, Dartmoor Public Park unfurls like a magical scene straight out of a storybook. Imagine yourself meandering in the midst of antiquated stone circles, looking at rock pinnacles outlined against the sky, and taking in the new aroma of wildflowers. Dartmoor is a haven for explorers, cyclists, and nature sweethearts, offering miles of trails that lead to stowed valleys, peaceful waterways, and all encompassing perspectives.

Devon's Waterfront Charms

Devon's shoreline is a mother lode of sandy sea shores, tough precipices, and enchanting coastline towns that coax with their interesting charm. Visit Exmouth for its broad sandy seashores and energetic waterfront, or investigate Sidmouth with its exquisite Rule design and beautiful beachfront strolls. Dawlish, known for its pleasant seafront and famous dark swans, offers a quiet retreat where you can loosen up and absorb the seaside landscape.

Verifiable Gems

Step back in time with visits to Exeter's noteworthy milestones and legacy locales. Investigate the underground sections that once filled in as middle age water channels underneath the city, giving an entrancing look into Exeter's past. Close by, Powderham Castle remains as a demonstration of Devon's privileged history, displaying stupendous engineering, wonderful nurseries, and exceptionally old fortunes that transport guests to another time.

Family-Accommodating Fun

For families, Exeter's environmental elements guarantee an abundance of exercises to engage and instruct. Go to Paignton Zoo for a very close experience with colorful creatures from around the world, or bounce on board the South Devon Rail route for a nostalgic steam train venture through grand open country. Intelligent historical centers like RAMM (Royal Albert Memorial Museum) offer involved shows and connecting with shows that enamor guests, everything being equal, making finding out about history and culture an astonishing experience.

Culinary Delights

No investigation of Exeter's environmental elements would be finished without enjoying Devon's culinary joys. Go through pleasant towns and moving slopes to find nearby ranch shops offering craftsman cheeses, newly prepared merchandise, and privately created wines and juices. Come by enchanting coffee bars for a sample of Devonshire cream teas, complete with hand crafted scones and thickened cream, a quintessential English treat that ought not be missed.

Uncovering Exeter's encompassing marvels welcomes you to set out on an excursion of revelation, where regular magnificence, rich history, and warm neighborliness anticipate. Exeter's road trips and trips vow to leave you enlivened and revived. Thus, pack your feeling of miracle, accumulate your friends and family, and set out to uncover the enchanted that anticipates just past Exeter's city limits.

13. NEARBY ATTRACTIONS

DISCOVERING GEMS NEAR EXETER

Simply a short distance from Exeter, a mother lode of unexpected, yet invaluable treasures anticipates energetic wayfarers. Whether you're a neighborhood looking for new experiences or a guest hoping to reveal the district's privileged insights, these close by attractions vow to please with their normal excellence, verifiable importance, and one of a kind appeal.

1. Killerton House and Gardens

Settled in the peaceful open country, Killerton House is a Georgian manor encompassed by dazzling nurseries and parkland. Investigate the stupendous insides of the house, which grandstand a rich assortment of verifiable relics and works of art. Outside, wander through arranged gardens, antiquated forests, and pleasant plantations that burst into variety with occasional blossoms.

2. Crealy Amusement Park and Resort

Ideal for families and daredevils the same, Crealy Amusement Park offers a day of energy with its variety of rides, attractions, and live shows. From delicate rides for the little ones to adrenaline-siphoning exciting rides, there's something for everybody to appreciate. Expand your encounter with a stay at the retreat, complete with lodges, setting up camp offices, and diversion choices for a sensational escape.

3. Exmouth Ocean side and Jurassic Coast

Simply a short drive from Exeter lies Exmouth, a waterfront town flaunting a staggering ocean side and admittance to the Jurassic Coast World Legacy Site. Go through a day relaxing on the sandy shores, building sandcastles with the family, or investigating the stone pools overflowing with marine life. For the bold, leave on a waterfront stroll to observe stunning perspectives on precipices, ocean stacks, and old fossils implanted in the stones.

4. Bicton Park Botanical Gardens

Escape into a natural wonderland at Bicton Park, home to more than 60 sections of land of wonderfully finished nurseries, lakes, and forests. Walk around themed gardens overflowing with extraordinary plants, visit the Victorian Palm House with its great assortment of exotic species, or investigate the serene field on a smaller than expected railroad ride. Bicton Park offers a quiet retreat for nature sweethearts and nursery devotees.

5. Dawlish Warren Nature Reserve

For untamed life lovers and bird watchers, Dawlish Warren Nature Save is a safe house of biodiversity situated along the dazzling South Devon coast. Stroll along the sandy spit, hills, and salt swamps to recognize uncommon case species, including relocating waders and occupant wildfowl. The save additionally offers potential open doors for picnicking, beachcombing, and getting a charge out of all encompassing perspectives on the shoreline.

Investigating the jewels close to Exeter discloses a universe of different encounters, from noteworthy manors and amusement parks to beachfront retreats and greenhouses. These close by attractions welcome you to set out on important excursions and make enduring recollections with friends and family. In this way, pack your feeling of interest and set out on a roadtrip to find the secret fortunes standing by past Exeter's city limits.

ITINERARIES FOR UNFORGETTABLE DAY TRIPS

Planning a day trip from Exeter? Here are some exciting itineraries to help you make the most of your time exploring nearby attractions. Whether you're interested in history, nature, or family fun, these day trips promise unforgettable experiences and lasting memories.

1. Historical Delights: *Killerton House and Exmouth*
- *Morning*: Start your day with a visit to Killerton House. Explore the grand Georgian mansion and its impressive collection of art and antiques. Take a leisurely stroll through the beautifully landscaped gardens and enjoy the peaceful surroundings.

- *Lunch*: Head to a local pub or cafe near Killerton for a traditional Devonshire lunch.

- *Afternoon*: Drive to Exmouth, a charming coastal town just a short distance away. Spend the afternoon relaxing on the sandy beach, exploring the town's shops and cafes, or taking a boat trip along the Jurassic Coast.

- **Evening**: Enjoy dinner at a seaside restaurant in Exmouth, with stunning views of the sunset over the water.

2. Family Adventure: *Crealy Theme Park and Dawlish Warren*
- ***Morning***: Kick off your day with a visit to Crealy Theme Park & Resort. Enjoy thrilling rides, live shows, and interactive exhibits that entertain kids and adults alike.

- ***Lunch***: Grab lunch at one of Crealy's dining options or pack a picnic to enjoy in the park.

- ***Afternoon***: Head to Dawlish Warren Nature Reserve, a short drive away. Explore the coastal dunes and salt marshes, spot wildlife and birds, and take a leisurely walk along the beach.

- **Evening**: End your day with an ice cream treat at Dawlish Warren and watch the sunset over the sea.

3. **Nature Escapade: *Dartmoor National Park and Bicton Park Botanical Gardens***
- *Morning*: Embark on a scenic drive to Dartmoor National Park. Spend the morning hiking or walking along one of the many trails. Discover ancient stone circles, wild ponies, and panoramic views of the moors.

- *Lunch*: Stop at a local pub or cafe in a nearby Dartmoor village for a hearty lunch.

- ***Afternoon:*** Visit Bicton Park Botanical Gardens, known for its stunning landscapes and diverse plant collections. Explore themed gardens, enjoy a ride on the miniature railway, and relax by the tranquil lakes.

- **Evening**: Return to Exeter, stopping for a delicious dinner at a countryside pub on the way back.

4. Coastal Charm: ***Exmouth Beach and Sidmouth***
- ***Morning***: Begin your day with a visit to Exmouth Beach. Enjoy a leisurely stroll along the promenade, build sandcastles on the beach, or try your hand at water sports.

- ***Lunch:*** Have lunch at a beachside cafe in Exmouth, savoring fresh seafood and local specialties.

- ***Afternoon:*** Drive to Sidmouth, a picturesque town known for its Regency architecture and scenic coastal walks. Explore the town's shops, visit the Jurassic Coast Information Centre, or relax in the tranquil Connaught Gardens.

- ***Evening:*** Head back to Exeter, stopping for a seaside dinner in Exmouth or Sidmouth to watch the evening sun dip below the horizon.

These itineraries offer a variety of experiences for every interest, whether you're seeking history, nature, family fun, or coastal charm. Customize your day trip from Exeter with these suggestions and create unforgettable memories exploring the nearby attractions. Enjoy the journey and immerse yourself in the beauty and diversity of Devon's countryside and coastline.

PART 6:
PRACTICALITIES

14. ESSENTIAL TIPS FOR VISITORS

HANDY ADVICE FOR A SMOOTH STAY

Arranging an outing to Exeter? Whether you're hanging around for a short visit or a more drawn out stay, capitalizing on your time includes a couple of straightforward tips to guarantee everything goes without a hitch. From exploring the city to getting a charge out of neighborhood conveniences, here's useful guidance to assist you with having a peaceful and pleasant experience.

1. Plan Ahead

Before you set out on the journey, set aside some margin to design your agenda and explore the attractions you need to visit. Check opening times, ticket costs, and any exceptional occasions or shows that might be going on during your visit. This will assist you with capitalizing on your time and keep away from frustration.

2. Get to Know the City
 Find out more about Exeter's layout and transportation choices. The downtown area is reduced and effectively walkable, yet open transports and cabs are likewise accessible for longer distances or on the other hand on the off chance that you don't really want to walk. Consider downloading a guide or utilizing a route application to assist you with getting around.

3. Embrace the Nearby Culture
　 Find an opportunity to submerge yourself in Exeter's rich culture and legacy. Visit neighborhood exhibition halls, craftsmanship displays, and authentic milestones to find out about

the city's set of experiences and customs. Remember to investigate the neighborhood markets, where you can test local rarities and get one of a kind trinkets to recollect your outing by.

4. Dress for the Weather

Exeter's weather conditions can be capricious, so be ready for all circumstances. Pack layers that you can undoubtedly add or eliminate contingent upon the temperature, and remember to be happy with strolling shoes for investigating the city and encompassing regions.

5. Remain Connected

Guarantee you approach correspondence and data all through your visit. Check assuming your convenience offers Wi-Fi or on the other hand in the event that there are public areas of interest accessible. Consider buying a neighborhood SIM card for your telephone in the event that you really want to settle on decisions or access the web while you're making the rounds.

6. Remain Safe and Secure

While Exeter is by and large a protected city, it's dependably shrewd to play it safe to safeguard yourself and your possessions. Keep your assets secure, know about your environmental factors, and observe any nearby wellbeing rules or suggestions.

7. Appreciate Neighborhood Cuisine

One of the most mind-blowing pieces of voyaging is attempting new food sources. Exeter offers an assortment of feasting choices, from conventional English bars serving good dinners to global eateries offering flavors from around the world. Feel free to wander outside of what might be expected and investigate neighborhood diners for a sample of legitimate Devonshire cooking.

8. Be Adaptable and Have Fun

Recollect that movement is an undertaking. Be adaptable with your arrangements, embrace unforeseen open doors, and partake in each snapshot of your visit in Exeter. Whether you're investigating verifiable milestones, loosening up in green spaces, or basically absorbing the nearby climate, capitalize on your visit and make recollections that will endure forever.

By following these convenient tips, you can guarantee a smooth and pleasant stay in Exeter, capitalizing on all that this lively city brings to the table. Safe ventures and live it up investigating Exeter and its environmental factors!

PRACTICAL INFORMATION TO KEEP IN MIND

While you're visiting another city like Exeter, having some functional data convenient can truly help you explore and partake in your visit without limit. Here is a manual for guarantee your excursion is smooth and calm:

1. Money and Payments

In Exeter, the money utilized is the British Pound (£). Most places acknowledge significant credit and check cards, yet it's in every case great to have some money on you for more modest buys or puts that don't take cards. You can trade cash at banks or use ATMs around the city.

2. Climate and What to Pack

The climate in Exeter can be eccentric, so it's ideal to check the figure before you pack. Summers are typically gentle, however downpour showers are normal, so pack a light waterproof coat or umbrella for good measure. Winters can be crisp, so bring layers and a comfortable coat on the off chance that you're visiting during the colder months.

3. Getting Around

Exeter is not difficult to get around with its dependable public vehicle framework. Transports are an incredible method for investigating the city and nearby attractions. You can likewise stroll around the downtown area, as many spots are inside strolling distance. For longer excursions, consider leasing a vehicle or utilizing trains, which associate Exeter to different urban communities and towns in Devon.

4. Opening times and Holidays

Many shops, attractions, and eateries in Exeter have explicit opening times. A few puts might be shut on Sundays or occasions, so it's smart to check quite a bit early, particularly if there's some place explicitly you need to visit. Plan your day as needed to take full advantage of your time.

5. Emergency Contacts

If there should be an occurrence of crises, dial 999 for police, fire, or clinical help. For non-crises or to report wrongdoing, you can contact the nearby police headquarters. It's likewise really smart to have your convenience's contact subtleties convenient for any neighborhood counsel or help you could require.

6. Local Etiquette and Customs

Exeter, similar to a large part of the UK, values good manners and regard. It's generally expected to welcome individuals courteously and line persistently in shops. Tipping is valued in cafés, typically around 10-15% in the event that a help charge is excluded. Smoking is denied in most indoor public spots.

7. Wi-Fi and Web Access

Numerous lodgings, bistros, and eateries in Exeter offer free Wi-Fi for clients. In the event that you want steady web access, consider getting a neighborhood SIM card with information or checking assuming your convenience gives solid network access.

8. Health and Safety

Exeter is by and large protected, yet it's wise to avoid potential risk like you would in any city. Watch out for your possessions, particularly in jam-packed regions. For clinical necessities, there are drug stores (called physicists) where you can move past-the-counter prescriptions. In the event of difficult ailment or injury, there are emergency clinics and clinical focuses accessible.

By remembering these pragmatic tips, you'll be good to go to partake in your time in Exeter. Whether you're hanging around for touring, shopping, or simply unwinding, these tips will assist with guaranteeing a smooth and pleasant visit. Live it up investigating all that Exeter brings to the table!

15. SUSTAINABLE TRAVEL IN EXETER

SUPPORTING RESPONSIBLE TOURISM INITIATIVES

As explorers, we have the ability to have a constructive outcome on the spots we visit, including delightful objections like Exeter. Supporting the travel industry drives isn't just useful for the climate and nearby networks yet in addition advances our own movement encounters. Here are a reasonable ways of participating in dependable tourism while investigating Exeter:

Pick Eco-Accommodating Accommodations

Settle on lodgings, guesthouses, or quaint little inns that focus on supportability. Search for facilities that execute energy-saving practices, utilize inexhaustible assets, and limit squander. Numerous eco-accommodation facilities in Exeter take part in reusing projects and backing neighborhood protection endeavors.

Regard Neighborhood Culture and Traditions

Carve out opportunities to find out about Exeter's social legacy and regard nearby traditions. Draw in with neighborhood craftsmans, visit authentic locales with worship, and backing conventional organizations. By getting it and valuing the nearby culture, you add to its protection and guarantee that people in the future can likewise partake in these remarkable customs.

Diminish Your Carbon Footprint

Limit your effect on the climate by picking reasonable transportation choices. Walk or cycle at whatever point conceivable to investigate Exeter's beguiling roads and parks. Utilize public vehicles like transports or trains for longer excursions, which decreases discharges contrasted with driving alone. Consider carpooling or leasing cross breed or electric vehicles assuming you want greater adaptability.

Support Neighborhood Organizations and Products

Embrace Exeter's dynamic nearby economy by shopping at free stores, markets, and craftsmans' slows down. Buy trinkets and presents that are privately made, supporting the vocations of craftspeople and decreasing the carbon impression related with imported products. Appreciate feasts at cafés that source fixings locally, advancing provincial agribusiness and lessening food miles.

Monitor Water and Energy

Practice capable utilization by moderating water and energy during your visit. Clean up, switch out lights and gadgets when not being used, and take part in towel and cloth reuse programs presented by facilities. Little activities on the whole add to saving Exeter's normal assets for people in the future.

Partake in Local area and Preservation Projects

Draw in with neighborhood local area drives or preservation projects that advance ecological stewardship and backing reasonable improvement in Exeter. Volunteer your time or give to associations attempting to safeguard natural life living spaces, keep up with trails, or teach the general population about preservation endeavors nearby.

Instruct Yourself and Others

Remain informed about reasonable travel practices and offer your insight with individual explorers. Urge others to embrace mindful tourism propensities by showing others how it's done and pushing for moral travel decisions. Together, we can establish a positive effect on Exeter's current circumstance, economy, and local area strength.

Supporting responsible tourism drives in Exeter isn't just about decreasing our impression; it's tied in with leaving a positive heritage for future guests and local people the same. Travel capably and guarantee that Exeter stays an inviting and reasonable objective for a long time into the future.

ECO-FRIENDLY PRACTICES FOR CONSCIOUS TRAVELERS

Venturing out to Exeter offers a brilliant chance to investigate while likewise being aware of our effect on the climate. Embracing eco-accommodating practices protects the magnificence of Exeter as well as supports feasible tourism endeavors. Here are reasonable tips for cognizant voyagers hoping to lessen their ecological impression:

1. Pick Green Accommodations

Settle on eco-accommodating lodgings, guesthouses, or get-away rentals that focus on supportability. Search for accreditations like Green Key or eco-names showing energy-proficient practices, squander decrease drives, and utilization of sustainable assets. These facilities frequently utilize measures, for example, energy-saving lights, water-saving apparatuses, and reusing programs.

2. *Limit Plastic Waste*

Pack reusable things, for example, water bottles, shopping sacks, and utensils to decrease single-utilize plastic utilization. Top off your water bottle from drinking fountains or request that cafés fill it for you. Try not to utilize expandable cutlery and straws, and pick eco-accommodating choices produced using bamboo or hardened steel if vital.

3. *Support Neighborhood and Natural Products*

Investigate Exeter's business sectors and shops to find privately developed or delivered merchandise. Pick cafés that focus on privately obtained fixings, supporting provincial ranchers and decreasing fossil fuel byproducts related with food transportation. Think about visiting ranchers' business sectors to buy new organic products, vegetables, and distinctive items, encouraging an association with the neighborhood local area.

4. Utilize Maintainable Transportation

Walk or cycle at whatever point conceivable to investigate Exeter's downtown area and close by attractions. Public transportation choices, for example, transports and trains are eco-accommodation options in contrast to driving, diminishing fossil fuel byproducts and gridlock. On the off chance that leasing a vehicle is essential, choose an eco-friendly or half breed vehicle and carpool with individual explorers to limit natural effect.

5. Regard Regular Natural surroundings and Wildlife

While visiting parks, nature holds, or waterfront regions around Exeter, practice responsible tourism by regarding untamed life living spaces and regular scenes. Remain on assigned trails, abstain from upsetting untamed life, and shun littering. Partake in coordinated eco-visits or directed strolls that advance natural mindfulness and preservation endeavors.

6. Save Water and Energy

Save assets during your visit by washing up, switching out lights and hardware when not being used, and partaking in towel and cloth reuse programs presented by facilities. Be aware of water utilization, particularly in areas inclined to dry season, and report any releases or water waste to the board.

7. Instruct Yourself and Others

Remain informed about neighborhood natural issues and preservation drives in Exeter. Draw in with occupants, local area experts, or progressives to find out about endeavors to safeguard normal territories, advance feasible the travel industry, and protect social legacy. Share your insight and encounters with companions and individual explorers to rouse positive change and energize dependable travel rehearses.

By taking on eco-accommodating works during your visit to Exeter, you add to safeguarding its normal excellence, supporting neighborhood networks, and advancing feasible tourism. Each little exertion combines with making an all the more naturally cognizant travel insight, guaranteeing that people in the future can keep on partaking in the marvels of Exeter. We should travel dependably and leave a positive effect on the spots we visit.

16. CONCLUSION

As you prepare to bid farewell to Exeter, take a moment to cherish the memories of your journey through this charming city. Your adventure here has been filled with discoveries, delights, and perhaps a few surprises along the way. Exeter has left its mark on you in unique ways.

Looking Back on Your Exeter Journey

Remember the quiet moments spent wandering through the historic streets, where every cobblestone seemed to whisper stories of centuries past. Reflect on the awe-inspiring architecture of Exeter Cathedral, standing tall as a testament to the city's enduring spirit. Recall the joy of exploring local markets, sampling Devonshire delights, and discovering hidden gems tucked away in cozy corners.

Farewell to Exeter

As you pack your bags and prepare to leave, know that Exeter will hold a special place in your heart. The warmth of its people, the beauty of its landscapes, and the richness of its culture have touched you in ways that only a journey can. Take with you not just souvenirs and photographs, but the memories of laughter shared with newfound friends and the peace found in quiet moments of reflection.

Until We Meet Again:

Though your time in Exeter may be coming to an end, remember that this farewell is not forever. Whether you return to revisit familiar haunts or explore new adventures, Exeter will always welcome you back with open arms. Until then, carry the spirit of Exeter with you—the spirit of exploration, discovery, and appreciation for the simple pleasures in life.

As you embark on your next adventure, may the memories of Exeter inspire you to seek beauty, embrace history, and treasure every moment along the way. Farewell, Exeter, until we meet again on the path of travel and discovery. Safe travels, and may your journey be filled with endless possibilities and the joy of new experiences.

Made in United States
Troutdale, OR
12/18/2024

26815596R00086